Little Book of Poems
By Peter William Percival Turner

First Edition
Forward Press Ltd 1998

Second Edition
Published by Richard Good 2021

© Peter William Percival Turner 1998

Printed in the UK by Amazon
50 Marlow Drive, Haywards Heath, RH16 3SH
Email: publishing@richardgood.co.uk

ISBN: 9798493979354

View From A Quill

Whom, will picketh up thy quill,
    Writeth that literature of prime
That which my soul doth thrill,
    Reminiscent of olden time
When Shelley's Cloud floated...
    o'er Wordsworth's Daffodil,
When Poets could make two lines rhyme?

Mine, grey matter, the brain.
    Understandeth not, the patter
Of modern day refrain,
    They writeth, of things complex!
Of anarchy, drink, drugs and sex.
    Use words absurd, begin with F and S
Endeth with G and T!
    Pray, is this the end of Poetry?

Oh! Heed ye whom lift the quills ...
    Tap the key..
Kill off the Daffodils.
    Pray hear my plea
If you can?
    Please, write Poems that rhyme
Poems that scan,
    That please the soul
Of this ill literate man!
    Poems of measure, Poems of pleasure,
Such toil, to lessen
    Shelley's turnings beneath the soil!

Dreaming Drifting

Dreaming... drifting... sweet inspiration,
    My spirit lifting . . . filled with elation..
Lifting my pen today...
    To write of the beauty of a Sussex way.
A view from a quill,
    A view from a hill.

I go gently... placidly in my tread –
    Enthralled by the beauty of Beachy Head.
The sea runs across the rocks ...
    Wetting my shoes, my socks.
It kisses the feet of those Sisters too...
    The magnificent Seven. Heaven! I view.

A child with delight, stoops whoops, young old,
    As creatures of the sea unfold...
Crabs, cockles and mussels alive oh!.
    Oh! am I alive with this splendour below!

Ozone wafting... gulls screaming –
    Sand shifting.. sun gleaming -
Drifting am I... to some other Sussex part,
    Inspired is my peaceful heart.

Peace Means to Me

P ondering... upon a countryside scene.

E nriched by sky of blue, tints of green,

A ffection for my restless heart.

C aptivated, by the glory of a peaceful part.

E nlivened, as I tread... this Sussex sod.

M agnificent! Here I feel, the very presence of my God.

E ntrusted. Surely, He today has done His duty.

A pocalypse! What of this world to come? Ugliness, beauty?

N oise of bomb, land mine, gun?

S ouls bedevilled by hate, war, despair, none!

T hat is not the sound
    I wish to hear,

O h no! Only laughter of children at play, bird song,
    in my ear,

M ediation, in places of unrest,
    meditation, in this lovely part.

E ureka! Eureka! The Peace of God and heart.

Satisfaction Replay, Fast Forward

Looking back, on glorious summer days.
    I reflect on the lovely times I had,
        exploring, filming Sussex ways.
The beauty of a country path....
    a leafy lane...
      Where wildflowers grow,
        dance gaily in a summer breeze...
Where birdsong, echoes from the trees.
    Of woodland glades where cuckoos sing...
Of rocky pools where limpets cling.

Looking back. The part I love
    Is upon the Downs way up above,
Looking down on all below...
    The villages, hamlets, where thatched roofs grow.
Away from congested town, busy road,
    Standing upon some Sussex hill
        where sheep may safely graze...
Where like them to,
    upon the landscape, I can gaze...
        Enthralled, enchanted, by the glory of god
That made the splendour of this Sussex sod.

Looking forward to summer's return
    Filming the subject for which I yearn.
One so very dear to me.
    The beauty of lovely Sussex,
        Sussex-By-The-Sea.

The Seven Sisters

This Heaven here, enthrals me, bliss.
    Sea laps my feet..
Encircling above, seagulls, I love.
    Venturing onto the rocks below,
Enduring soggy socks and shoes, who cares?
    Never, have I seen such a splendid show..

Sisters, their mantles of white, toupees of green,
    Indeed, splendour beyond compare,
        the magnificent seven here.

Spellbound by the beauty
    where the downs meet the sea,
The ever-changing faces of sisters
    battered by ravaging storm...
Everlasting, but the undercutting of the sea.
    causes their ever-changing form.
    Rock pools, delight little her or he

Searching.. for those creatures of the sea.
    Satisfied, with peaceful heart, I shake God's hand
And thank Him for this beauty grand.

Rambling Prose

R ambling,

A round, about...

M akes me shout.

B eautiful, is this place.

L oving each, and every view.

I mmanent, inherent of God's prevailing universe.

N othing has earth to show more fair,

G od, I see in all this beauty here.

P raise bel for all this glory that I see..

R ambling, such delight,
    seeing the joy of a Sussex sight,

O f clambering over rocks, children searching...
    for creatures of the sea.

S etting of the sun, on silver shimmering sea,
    such splendour to me.

E vening has come, time to depart...
    aching back, blistered feet, but peaceful heart.

Hand Held

The sky is grey, I really
    like it blue,
When I come to film a lovely view.
However, it may well clear,
    And through the clouds, a hole appear,
So lovely sun comes shining down...
    My beaming face replaces frown.

What is this ozone that we hear about?
    Is it nay, a hole in heaven
        letting sunshine out?
The ozone and heaven, are here with me,
    It is the Oh! I exclaim
        when this beauty I see.

Leaving rat-race town... do I begrudge?
    Where its noisy, busy streets I'd trudge. ...
Oh no! this lovely amble... ramble, leisurely stroll
    Through woodland glade, thicket bramble,
        revives my soul.

These pathways which I tread... this sod,
    Have, and has today, been trodden by God..
He has surely walked this way.
    His glory I see in grandiose array
Why! I think He even holds
    my hand, today!

Chanctonbury Ring

C lumped
H igh above,
A lovely view.
N ow, new saplings grow,
C ircle of trees, Gorings show.
T rees, a few, many taken away,
O ctober day, eighty-seven, in hurricane blow.
N ow they grow again to see another day,
B eautiful! Shade for the walkers.
    of the South Downs Way.
U p here, ring of trees, Lord Goring's
    dream come true,
R azed, reborn. Mother Goring's got her cap
    on a misty day.
Y es, that's what the folk of bygone times
    would say, you know.

R ing of mist. It was her cap you see, I remember it well.
I n month of May, the Morris men dance... bringing in
    the wondrous, glorious summer.
N ew life, for flowers that grow this way, cowslips,
    daffodils, primroses, they sure look swell.
G row, this Ring for which I applaud, May the circle be
    unbroken, Praise The Lord!

Blest In Peace

Do I hold a seashell to my ear
    the sea to hear?
Oh no! for I behold the beauty
    of its flow...
As it runs across the rocks ...
    wetting shoes and socks,
Kissing the feet of those Sisters too,
Such a splendid view.

Cockles and mussels. Alive, alive oh!
Am I alive with this beautiful show.
Beauty up for grabs, and crabs that nestle
    in rocky pools, doing sideway crawls.
Pools, in which, seaweed green, brown, red,
Bobs up and down, like the ringlets
    on a mermaid's head.

Oh! Oh! Heaven. A view to a thrill,
    are the magnificent seven.
The Sisters, standing hand in hand,
Their mantles of white, toupees of green.
Such a pretty scene to me.
    where the Downs meet the sea.
Shingle slithers to and fro
    with the waters flow,
Splashing, dashing, sometimes crashing.
Smashing is the tranquillity, pure bliss.
Salty spray, lands upon my lips, the bows of ships,
Tingling like the tingle that flows from head to toes.
God! am I enthralled with this glorious show!
Could this be the nearest thing to heaven
    I shall ever see?
For some despairing soul, it is R.I.P.

Ah! No Car So

Ah no car so! Tranquillity, peace!
    No noise of motoring machine,

Car! It's a happy release.
    So splendid is this coastal scene,

Far away from the maddening crowd.
    The busy world is hushed,

No unwelcome sound to becloud,
    I ramble on, unrushed.

Sea laps the feet of Sisters proud.
    I feel the breeze... my face, brushed.

Hear, the gulls screaming...
    Such beauty, at this lovely part.

Am, am I dreaming? heart.
    Oh no! Tranquillity, peace of mind, soul,

Glimpses Of Glory

G ladsome, am I today,

L oving my ramble, around a Sussex way.

I lluminated, is my face!

M ajestic, is the beauty of this place. P re-eminent here, this Sussex fair,

S howing me its splendour beyond compare..

E xploring here, there, some hidden part,

S ongbirds, warm cockled heart.

O h! Sussex. I love you so,

F or time when bluebells, daffodils grow

G iving me the joy of their splendid display.

L ovely, dancing, waving in a gentle sway.

O h! Sussex. I adore your rocky shore,

R ambling on rocks... seeing the beauty in store.

Y et weary with aching blistered part,
    You give to me... a peaceful heart.

Untitled

Sea, glistening. Me, listening.
    Seagulls screaming. Sun gleaming.
Sand shifting. Spirit lifting.
    Shingle slithers. Little rivers.

Little maid. Bucket, spade.
    Digging sand. Castle grand.
Wind, blowing. Gale showing.
    Sea rushing. Castle crushing.

Maid scowling. Wind howling.
    Waves crashing. She's dashing.
Storm subsides. White horse rides.
    Once more. Peaceful shore.

Drifting And Dreaming

Floating in a sky of blue
    With white fluffy clouds, passing by.
This feller, with funny umbrella,
    Draws attention to my eye.
He is an easy rider,
    No! he is not on a hang-glider,
With that great big umbrella,
    Billowing above his head,
He is parascending instead.
Surely, his world he has upon a string?
    Well, strings quite a few
As he drifts and floats up above,
    Enjoying the view.
The wind, brushes against his face...
    As he observes the beauty of this place.
Rising and falling, with each current of air.
    Oh! It must be just like heaven
        way up there!
I wish it was me.
    But to be honest,
I have encountered heaven with these paths
    I have trod, you see.
I will leave these folk to drift
    to dream...
Above this Sussex course.
    I will be jolly glad, it's not me,
        that has landed in the gorse!
Gone off track, to be greeted by cows
    With a pat on the back!
Now I must fly...
    Well, set off in my stride...
There is so much more beauty
    Waiting for me,
Here in this lovely county
    Of Sussex, Sussex-By-The-Sea.

Devils Dyke

D evil

E vil being.

V isited this place.

I ncensed, by churches below,

L onged to flood the show.

S hovelled earth towards the sea.

D isturbed, by St Cuthman visiting lady nearby.

Y es! Candlelight, frightened devil off into night.

K now ye, that God walks here now it's true.

E verlasting, showing us His handy work, glory of the lovely view.

~~~

The Cloud

I wandered lonely...
    As a cloud of monoxide fumes
Floated on by, o'er vales and hills...
    When all at once,
I saw a crowd of blackened blooms.
    A ghost of Wordsworth Daffodils.
Beside the motorways, beneath the trees.
    Coughing, spluttering in the wheeze.

Glory Day on A Sussex Way

G randeur, is the picture I secure.

L andscapes, seascapes, I really love.

O f lovely Sussex, such are my demure.

R ambling. the Belloc line, the Downs above.

Y es! Satisfaction, replayed in my viewer.

D elighted am I, as horses pass by, trot..

A mazed at the splendour of the Weald below:

Y es! Captivated by the glory of God, besot.

O n I trek at easy pace -

N estled below, Ditchling where writers, musicians,
   singers abound,

A nd who knows? Maybe, poets too?

S o beautiful the view, the shades of green
   the sky of blue, hardly a sound.

U p here along the track, are windmills two,

S tanding side-by-side, Jack and Jill.

S he fell down! Restored by volunteers,
   she stands anew.

E ncompassed by this Down land beauty
   she goes round.

X cellent place, for ramblers to stop for cup of brew.

W alkers, Horse riders, bikers, joggers, eastwards,
westwards bound.

A stounded by this glory, God founded,
   I would say it's true,

Y es! this lovely part, heart of Sussex,
   The King of Glory, crowned!

Autumn's Tints, Winter's Hints

The sound of rustling, crackling leaves, underfoot.
    Autumn has arrived, the trees are going kaput.
The coats of green, that they proudly wore,
    Are no more.
Falling... fluttering... without a sound,
    They lie in tatters on the ground.

The trees stand naked, in cold night air
    Surrounded by that coat they proudly wore,
Discarded... like some garment
    On a child's bedroom floor.
Leaves, red, brown, orange, yellow,
    with a tint of gold,
Worn by those trees so bold
With their ivy, moss-covered barks,
    Trees, under which lovers would have their larks!
One of the pleasures of being a tree,
    Until the knife goes in ...
Arrowed heart, T loves D.

In winter's gales, they bend and sway,
    Ride out the stormy blast,
Sticky buds, start to appear.
    Another winter's past.
Spring is knocking on the door...
    The trees put on that coat they wore
Then we can all agree
    That, there is nothing lovelier than a tree.

West Pier

This empty shell for which bell tolls,
    Holds, only memories of Victorian times.
Of bustled dress and parasols,
    Of candyfloss, and Brighton rock.
Storms, angry seas swell,
    Has taken stock..

Folk, no longer do they flock,
    Where birds of the air now dwell,
In eves, rafters of old tyme music hall..
    They nest, they sing,
Backed by the sound of the sea below.
    No noise, the joys of piano, violin string.
Tea dances, quick, quick slow!

Haunting, daunting,
This beautiful architecture,
    Weather-beaten, eaten, rotted.
Now in state of imperfecture.
    For many, a pier once besotted.
Like so today, folk eager to save
    The grand old lady
From the depths of that watery grave.

Lottering With Intent!

No happy landings of fish today!
    Upon stage, rusted, broken away.
No casting line...
    All you hook in brine,
Submerged ironwork, barnacle encrusted,
    Girders, struts, rusted.
Flotsam and Jetsam,
    You would surely get some.

The only landings here,
    Seagulls, birds of the air,
Upon few remaining railings,
    Tossed, torn by sea's rage, wind's wailings...

Catch a view, ponder...
    Of Victorian architecture, none as fonder
As this pier of the best,
    Going west...!
Almost! not quite.
    Lottery money will put it right.

The scenes once more,
    Of penny machines, what the Butler saw?
Those glories of old.
    Tea dances, of fortunes told.
The future today, is looking good
    For this rusting hulk of rotting wood.

Paws For Thought.

Suddenly,
    Little fingers, entwine.
With mine.
    My hand grasped
By young, dainty hand clasped.

I look down
    To see a smiling face
Big eyes of brown.

You cannot explain
    What you wish to say!
You come from the Ukraine,
    A new girl in school today,
And yet,
    That little act
Of holding hands,
    Tells me that
We are all brothers, sisters, from whatever lands.

Yes! Actions speak louder than words, indeed,
    We are all joined together
Whatever race or creed.

Oliver's Twist!

There are lots of little Olivers in Africa.
    They never ask for 'more'!
They have not even tasted,
    That which comes before.

~~~

Food For Fraught

This banana, unbruised unpeeled,
    In bin, lies.
Sandwiches in cling film, untouched.
    That child starving,
Fragile limbs crutched, dies.
    This child 's mutter, 'Urg! Peanut butter"
That child in despair, lies in gutter.
    Another, hands clasped, as if in prayer.
No food is grasped, none to spare.

Banana, dies in sin! Rotting there,
    For is it not sin to dispose
When starving children, there are those?
    A peanut sandwich is very nice,
You do not like it, you dump it.
    Your brother, sister, pays the price!
Crying, dying.

In a country, impoverished
    Of low, or no means,
That child, would if it could
    Jump at the chance
To eat up your greens!

West Pier

Pitted, embittered, rotting to the shore.
Victorian Pier of charm, of beauty, sadly no more.
You had your day, you have come to harm.
As you rot, rust away.
No happy landings today.
For the stage is a sad and sorry state of decay.
Not looking at all grand.
Is this, where paddle steamer use to stand?
Now only Gulls, birds of the air, settle on its railings.
The few left there.
It is rickety, battered, it's a structure out of place.
Oh those memories of yester-year.
Bring smiles to my face.

There is music coming from the music hall
    that use to be.
It is the birds singing,
    to the sound of the sea.

Naked, rusted iron columns stand.
With memories of old,
    of penny machines, of fortunes told.
Columns, once more eager to carry the weight.
The sound of feet patter, of folk eager to win.
    Hear the clatter, as the coins tumble down.
See the silver balls whizzing round.
Kids posting a penny between the gap, to see it drown.
To poke head through hole,
        where clowns' heads are meant to be,
            smile please.
Ah the memories come flooding back,
    so very clear to me!

~~~

Simply captured.
The beauty of Sussex
Will leave you enraptured?
Wishing maybe to stand upon a hill,
A Sussex shore,
Of the beauty, have your fill.
A paradise found. You will want more
To stand and stare
At the glory of a God profound,
Awaiting there.

~~~

© 2021 Peter William Percival Turner
All Rights Reserved

Printed in Great Britain
by Amazon